ANDROCLES
THE LION

Adapted by

Aurand Harris

*This book
donated by
Harry Zimbler
PSU, MFA '83*

*A play for the young, based on the
Italian Tale of "Androcles and the
Lion," and written in the style of
Italian Commedia dell 'arte.*

Copyright, 1964, by
THE CHILDREN'S THEATRE PRESS

The Anchorage Press, Inc.
Post Office Box 8067
New Orleans, Louisiana 70182

ISBN Number 0-87602-105-4

ROYALTY NOTE

For
Stan Raiff
who first produced and directed
ANDROCLES AND THE LION

The following is a copy of the programme of the first performance of ANDROCLES AND THE LION, presented at the Forty-first Street Theatre in New York City, 7 December, 1963:

Expore, Inc. Presents

Stan Raiff's Production of

ANDROCLES AND THE LION

A Play With Music in the Style of
Commedia dell 'Arte

by

AURAND HARRIS

Directed by Stan Raiff

Musical Score	*Choreography*	*Costumes and Settings*
Glenn Mack	Beverly Schmidt	Richard Rummonds

ANDROCLES ....Joseph Barnaba

LION ....Richard Sanders

PANTALONE ....Leonard Josenhans

CAPTAIN...Eric Tavares

ISABELLA ....Jacqueline Coslow

LELIO ....Christopher McCall

Assistant Director: Montgomery Davis
Assistants to Mr. Rummonds: Maryet Ramsey and Charles MacNab

(Pictures used in this book were taken from this
production, and are reproduced here with the
permission of the photographer, Baruch Katz, of
New York City.)

4

ANDROCLES AND THE LION

CAST

ANDROCLES

PANTALONE

ISABELLA

LELIO

CAPTAIN

LION AND PROLOGUE

SCENE

The improvised stage of a Commedia dell'arte troupe
of strolling players. Sixteenth Century, Italy.

The play is in two parts.

MUSIC NOTE

The music for *Androcles and the Lion* covers a wide range of styles. In order to enhance the character of the Commedia dell' Arte form of the play, we chose to begin and end *Androcles* with music that is reminiscent of the early renaissance.

Thus, the Overture, Finale, and some of the incidental music utilize rythmic modes, short melodic fragments built from modal scales, and improvised percussion sounds executed by the players, on such instruments as hand drums, bells, and cymbals.

As each of the players is introduced, he is given a musical theme, to help emphasize his character in the play. Some of this material is then used in the songs.

The songs are simple, and were composed with the playwright's co-operation. Their purpose is to bring out the dramatic quality of various situations. They range from a work-song for Androcles, to a lament for Isabella, and a mock funeral march as the Captain and the Miser march Androcles into the pit.

There is also a chorus for everyone to sing. This, and the Lion's song, which end the first act, invite audience participation.

—Glenn R. Mack
New York City

Note to Producers

Distinguished original music for this play was composed for the New York production by Glenn R. Mack.

Complete piano score for the overture, seven songs, background music, and finale, is available at a fee of $17.50.

Conductor's score and parts for trumpet, flute, bassoon, drums, and harpsichord (piano, or prepared piano), is available at a fee of $20.00.

6

Scene from New York production of ANDROCLES AND THE LION

Scene from New York production of ANDROCLES AND THE LION

Scene from New York production of ANDROCLES AND THE LION

ANDROCLES AND THE LION

ACT ONE

(The curtains open on a bare stage with the cyclorama lighted in many colors. There is lively music and the Performers enter, playing cymbals, flute, bells, and drums. They are a Commedia dell'arte group.

Arlequin, dressed in his traditional bright patches, leads the parade. Next is Lelio and Isabella, the romantic forever young lovers. Next is Pantalone, the comic old miser. Next is the Captain, the strutting, bragging soldier. And last is the Prologue who wears a robe and who later plays the Lion.

After a short introductory dance, they line up at the footlights, a colorful troupe of comic players).

PROLOGUE. Welcome!
Short, glad, tall,
Big, sad, small,
Welcome all!

(Actors wave and pantomine "Hello").

We are a troupe of strolling players,
With masks, bells, and sword,

9

(Actors hold up masks, ring bells, and wave sword).

A group of comic portrayers
Who will act out upon the boards
A play for you to see—
A favorite tale of Italy,
Which tells how a friend was won
By a kindness that was done.
Our play is—"Androcles and the Lion."

(Actors beat cymbals, ring bells).

The players are: Arlequin—

(Arlequin steps forward).

Who will be Androcles, a slave.

(Arlequin bows, steps back, and Pantalone steps forward).

Pantalone, stingy and old.
Who thinks only of his gold.

(Pantalone holds up a bag of gold, bows, steps back; and Isabella and Lelio step forward and pose romantically).

Isabella and Lelio, two lovers
Whose hearts are pierced by Cupid's dart.

(They bow, step back, and Captain marches forward).

It is the bragging Captain's lot
To complicate the plot.

(Captain waves his wooden sword, bows, and steps back).

There is one more in our cast—
The Lion! He, you will see last.
Set the stage—

(Actors quickly set up small painted curtain backdrop).

Drape the curtains—raise the platform stand!
Here we will make a magic circle—
Take you to a magic land—
Where love is sung, noble words are spoken,
Good deeds triumph, and evil plots are broken.

(Holds up long scroll).

Our story is written on this scroll which I hold.
What happens in every scene here is told.

(Hangs scroll on proscenium arch at L).

Before we start, I will hang it on a hook
So if someone forgets his part
And has the need, he may have a look
And then proceed.

All the words in action or in song
We will make up as we go along.
All is ready! Players, stand within.

(Actors take places behind curtain).

For now I bow and say—the play—begins!

(He bows).

In ancient Rome our scene is laid,
Where the Emperor ruled and all obeyed.

(Points to curtain which is painted with a street in the middle and with a house on either side).

A street you see, two chariots wide,
With a stately house on either side.
In one lives Pantalone—rich, stingy, sour,

(Pantalone leans out the window-flap on the house at R and scowls).

Who counts and recounts his gold every hour.

(Pantalone disappears).

With him lives his niece Isabella, who each day

(Isabella leans out the window).

Looks lovingly—longingly—across the way

(Lelio leans out the window of the house at L).

At the other house, wh re Lelio lives, a noble sir, who looks across lovingly—longingly—at her.

(Lelio sighs loudly. Isabella sighs musically, and they both disappear. Androcles enters from R, around the backdrop with broom).

And all the while Androcles toils each day.
A slave has no choice but to obey.

(Prologue exits at R).

ANDROCLES *(Music. He sweeps comically, in front of the door, over the door, then down the "street" to footlights. SINGS).*

Up with the sun
My day begins.
Wake my Nose,
Shake my toes,
Hop and never stop.
No, never stop until I—
Off to the butcher's,
Then to the baker's,
To and from the sandalmaker's.

11

Hop and never stop.
No, never stop until I—
Spaghetti prepare
With sauce to please her.
Dust with care
The bust of Ceasar.
Hop and never stop.
No, Never stop until I—drop.

Some masters, they say, are kind and good. But mine . . .! He
cheats and he beats—he's a miser. Never a kind word does he
say, but shouts, "Be about it!" And hits you a whack on the back
to make sure. I'm always hungry. He believes in *under* eating.
I'm fed every day with a beating. I sleep on the floor by the door
to keep the robbers away. My clothes are patched and drafty because my master is stingy, and cruel, and crafty! When—oh when
will there ever be a Roman Holiday for me!

(SINGS).

Will my fortune always be,
Always be such drudgery?
Will hope ever be in my horoscope?
Oh, when will I be free?

PANTALONE *(Enters around R of backdrop, counting money)*.
. . . twenty-two, twenty-three, twenty-four, twenty-five . . .

*(Androcles creeps up behind him, and playing a trick, taps Pan-
talone on the back with broom. Pantalone jumps)*.

Who is there?

ANDROCLES. Androcles.

PANTALONE. Be about it! Be off! Go! Collect my rents for the day.
Everyone shall pay.

(Androcles starts R).

Lock the windows tight. Bolt the doors.

(Androcles starts L).

My stool! Bring me my stool.

(Androcles exits R).

Lazy stupid fool! There will be no supper for you tonight. Oh,
I will be buried a poor man yet—without a coin to put in my
mouth to pay for ferrying me across the River Styx.

(Androcles runs in R with stool).

My stool!

ANDROCLES *(Places stool behind Pantalone and pushes him down on
it roughly. Pantalone gasps in surprise)*.

12

Yes, my master.

PANTALONE. Go! Collect my rents. Make them pay. Bring me—my gold. Away!

ANDROCLES. Yes, oh master. I run!

(He starts "running" to L at top speed, then stops, looks back impishly, and then slowly walks).

PANTALONE *(Brings out bag and starts counting).*

Twenty-six, twenty-seven, twenty-eight, twenty-nine, thirty . . .

ISABELLA *(At the same time, she leans out the window, calls, stopping Androcles).*

Androcles . . . Androcles!

(He runs to her U.R. She gives him a letter).

For Lelio. Run!

(Androcles nods and smiles, pantomimes "running" to painted house on curtain at L, pantomimes knocking. There is music during the letter scene).

LELIO *(Appears at his window, takes letter).*

Isabella!

(Androcles smiles and nods. Lelio gives him a letter. Androcles "runs" to Isabella who takes letter).

ISABELLA. Admired!

(Gives Androcles another letter. He "runs" with leaps and sighs to Lelio who takes it).

LELIO. Adored!

(He gives Androcles another letter. He "runs" enjoying the romance, to Isabella who takes it).

ISABELLA. Bewitched!

(She gives him another letter—they are the same three sheets of parchment passed back and forth—which he delivers. This action is continued with a letter to each lover, and with Androcles "running" faster and faster between them).

LELIO. Bewildered!

ANDROCLES. And she has a dowry. The gold her father left her.

("Runs" to Isabella with letter).

ISABELLA. Enraptured!

LELIO. Inflamed!

13

ISABELLA. Endeared!

(Holds letter).

LELIO. My dear!

(Holds letter).

ANDROCLES. My feet!

(Androcles sinks exhausted to ground. Isabella and Lelio disappear behind the window flaps. Music stops).

PANTALONE *(Picks up the dialogue with his action, which has been continuous).*

. . . One hundred three, one hundred four, one hundred five, one hundred six . . .

(Bites a coin to make sure).

one hundred seven . . . one hundred . . .

LELIO *(Enters from L, around backdrop).* Signor Pantalone.

PANTALONE *(Jumps from stool in fear).* Someone is here!

LELIO. A word with you, I pray.

PANTALONE *(Nervously hides money).* What—what do you wish to say?

LELIO. I come to speak of love. I come to sing of love!

(Reads romantically from a scroll he takes from his belt).

"To Isabella."

PANTALONE. My niece?

LELIO. "Oh, lovely, lovely, lovely, lovely flower,
Growing lovelier, lovelier, lovelier every hour . . .
Shower me your petals of love, oh Isabella,
I stand outside—with no umbrella."
Signor, I ask you for Isabella. I ask you for her hand in marriage.

PANTALONE. Marry—Isabella?

LELIO *(Reads again).*

"My life, my heart, revolve about her,
Alas, I cannot live without her."

PANTALONE *(Happy at the prospect).* You will support her?

LELIO. I ask you—give me, Isabella.

(Pantalone nods gladly).

Give us your blessing.

(Pantalone nods eagerly and raises his hand).

14

Give her—her dowry.

PANTALONE *(Freezes)*. Money!

LELIO. The gold her father left her.

PANTALONE. Gold! It is mine—to keep for her.

LELIO. But hers when she marries.

PANTALONE. How did he find out? No. She shall not marry you. Never! Part with my gold! Help! Androcles!

(Androcles runs to him).

LELIO. Part with Isabella? Help! Androcles!

(Androcles, between them, runs from one to the other as their suffering increases).

PANTALONE. My heart is pounding.

LELIO. My heart is broken.

PANTALONE. Quick! Attend!

LELIO. Lend!

PANTALONE. Send!

LELIO. Befriend!

ANDROCLES *(To Lelio)*. There is hope.

PANTALONE. I am ill.

LELIO. Amend!

ANDROCLES *(To Lelio)*. Elope!

PANTALONE. I have a chill!

LELIO *(Elated with the solution)*. Transcend!

(Exits around L of backdrop).

PANTALONE. I will take a pill!

(Exits around R of backdrop).

ANDROCLES *(To audience)*. The end!

(Comes to footlights and SINGS).

They are my masters and I obey.
But who am I? I often say.
"Androcles!" They ring.
"Androcles!" I bring.
But who am I?
A name—I am a name they call,
Only a name—that's all.

(Speaks simply and touchingly).

15

My father's name was Androcles. We lived on a farm by the sea. Free to be in the sun—to work the land—to be a man. One day when my father was away, a ship came in the bay. "Pirates," my mother cried. I helped her and my sisters hide, but I was caught and brought to Rome—and sold—for twenty pieces of gold. I thought I would run away! But when they catch a slave they decree a holiday. The Emperor and everyone comes to watch the fun of seeing a run-away slave being beaten and eaten by a wild beast. Personally I don't feel like being the meal for a beast. So I stay . . . just a name . . .

(SINGS).

"Androcles!" They ring.
"Androcles!" I bring.
But who am I?
If I were free
Who would I be?
Maybe . . . maybe . . .
A doctor with a degree,
A poet, a priest, a sculptor, a scholar,
A senator—emperor with a golden collar!
I want to be free
So I can find—me.

PANTALONE *(Calls off, then enters U.R.).* Androcles! Androcles!

ANDROCLES. You see what I mean.

PANTALONE. Androcles!

ANDROCLES. Yes, my master.

PANTALONE. Quick! Answer the bell. Someone is at the gate.

(Androcles picks up stool and crosses to R).

Then come to me in the garden by the wall.

(Holds up a second bag of gold, different colors from the first).

I am going to bury—to plant—this bag of—stones.

ANDROCLES. Plant a bag of stones?

PANTALONE. Be off! To the gate!

(Androcles exits D.R. Pantalone holds up bag, schemingly).

Ah, inside this bag are *golden* stones! It is Isabella's dowry.

(There is a loud crashing of wood off R, announcing the entrance of the Captain).

Who is at the gate? I have forgot.

(Hurries to scroll hanging by the proscenium arch, reads—announcing in a loud voice).

16

"The Captain enters!"

CAPTAIN *(He struts in D.R., wooden sword in hand. His voice is as loud as his look is fierce).* Who sends for the bravest soldier in Rome? Who calls for the boldest Captain in Italy!

PANTALONE. I—Pantalone.

(Goes to him, speaks confidentially).

I will pay you well—

(Looks away. It breaks his heart).

—in gold—

(Then anxiously. Androcles peeks in at R).

to guard my niece. I have learned today she wishes to marry. You are to keep her lover away. Stand under her window. Station yourself at the door. Isabella is to be kept a prisoner forever more.

(No reaction from Captain).

ANDROCLES. A prisoner? She will be a slave—like me.

PANTALONE. What do you say?

CAPTAIN *(pompously).* I say—she who is inside is not outside.

ANDROCLES *(To audience).* I say—no one should be held a slave. This is treachery!

(Exits U.R. around backdrop).

CAPTAIN *(Struts).* I have guarded the royal Emperor. I have guarded the sacred temple. I can guard one niece—with one eye shut.

(Shuts one eye and marches L)

PANTALONE. No, no. The house is over there.

(Points R).

And that is her window.

(Isabella leans out of window).

CAPTAIN. Someone is there! Death to him when he tastes my sword!

(Advances with sword waving).

PANTALONE. No. No! It is she! *(Whispers).* It is—Isabella.

ISABELLA *(SINGS happily).*

Oh, yellow moon
Mellow moon
In the tree,
Look and see
If my lover
Waits for me.

17

PANTALONE *(Softly)*. Keep watch. Keep guard. She must not meet her lover.

(Captain salutes, clicks his heels, turns and with thundering steps starts to march. Androcles slips in from around backdrop U.L. and listens).

Sh!

(Captain marches with high, silent steps to window and stands at attention. Pantalone speaks to audience).

I must go to the garden! In this bag is the gold her father left her. I gave my oath to *keep* it—for her. To keep it safely—and for me. I will bury it deep, deep in the ground. Never to be found.

(He hurries off D.L.)

ANDROCLES *(To audience)*. More trickery that's wrong. The gold belongs to Isabella.

ISABELLA *(Aware someone is outside)*. Lelio?

CAPTAIN *(Laughs)*. Ha ha ha—no.

ISABELLA. Oh!

CAPTAIN. I am the Captain!

ISABELLA. Oh?

CAPTAIN. I guard your door. You cannot come or go.

ISABELLA. Oh.

CAPTAIN. Do not despair. I will keep you company. Observe how handsome I am—fifty women swooned today.

ISABELLA *(Calls softly)*. Lelio . . . ?

CAPTAIN. Know how brave I am—on my way to the barber two dragons I slew!

ISABELLA. Lelio . . . . . ?

CAPTAIN. Hear what a scholar I am—I say, "He who is sleeping is not awake."

ISABELLA. Lelio-o-o-o.

(Cries daintily. Captain makes a sweeping bow to her).

No!

(She disappears, letting the flap fall).

CAPTAIN. She sighs.

(Louder crying of musical "o's" is heard).

She cries. Ah, another heart is mine! Fifty-*one* women have swooned today!

(Poses heroically).

ANDROCLES. I must do something! She cannot be put in bondage. No one should be. Everyone should be free. But how—

(Beams with an idea, looks at scroll by proscenium arch and points).

Ah, look and see!

(He quickly reads scroll at side).

ISABELLA *(Appears at window, SINGS sadly).*

Oh lonely moon,
Only moon,
Do you sigh,
Do you cry
For your lover
As—as I?

ANDROCLES. Yes, here is the plan I need!

(Clasps hands and looks up in prayer).

Oh, gods of the temple, please give me the courage to succeed.

(Makes a grand bow to Captain).

Signor Captain!

(Captain jumps).

It is said you are so fierce the sun stops when you frown.

CAPTAIN. That is true.

(Makes a frightening frown, turns, and frightens Androcles).

ANDROCLES. And that the tide goes out whenever you sneeze.

CAPTAIN. That is true.

(Screws up his face comically, puffs up and up his chest, then sneezes).

A-a-a-achew!

ANDROCLES *(Circling in front of Captain, going to R, toward window).* Oh, brave and mighty Captain, I shake before you.

(Bows, back to audience, shaking).

CAPTAIN. Yesterday I swam five hundred leagues.

ANDROCLES. I heard you swam one thousand.

CAPTAIN. One thousand leagues I swam into the sea.

ANDROCLES. I heard it was into the ocean.

CAPTAIN. The ocean! To meet a ship—

19

ANDROCLES. A fleet of ships.

CAPTAIN. To meet a fleet of ships!

(Captain suddenly huffs and puffs as he starts pantomiming how he swam in the ocean, his arms pulling with great effort).

ANDROCLES *(At the same time, whispers to Isabella).* I have a plan to set you free, listen—carefully.

(Whispers, pointing to Captain. Pantomimes dropping handkerchief and fanning himself).

CAPTAIN *(Suddenly starts coughing and waving his arms).* Help! Help! I am drowning! Drowning!

ANDROCLES *(Rushes to him, hits him on back).* Save him. Throw out a rope. Man overboard!

CAPTAIN *(Sighs in relief, then dramatically continues with his adventure).* I was saved by a school of mermaids—beautiful creatures —and all of them swooned over me.

ANDROCLES. Then you swam on and on—

CAPTAIN *(Swimming on L, comically).* And on—

ANDROCLES *(Pushing him to exit).* And on—

CAPTAIN. And on—

ANDROCLES. And on—

CAPTAIN. And on—

(Exits L, "swimming").

ANDROCLES *(Quickly speaks to Isabella).* Do as I say and you can escape. We will trick the Captain. Wave your handkerchief. Get his attention. Then say the night is so warm—fan yourself. As he becomes warmer, he will shed his cap and hat and sword— and you will put them on. You will be the Captain.

ISABELLA. I?

ANDROCLES *(On his knees).* Try.

ISABELLA. The Captain's cape and hat will cover me, and I will be free to go—to Lelio.

CAPTAIN *(Re-enters at L).* After I had sunk the fleet of ships—

ANDROCLES. And brought the treasure back.

CAPTAIN. Treasure?

ANDROCLES. You awoke.

CAPTAIN. Awoke?

ANDROCLES. And found—it was but a dream.

(Isabella waves her handkerchief, then drops it coyly. Captain sees it and smiles seductively).

CAPTAIN. Ah! She signals for me to approach. Signora—your servant.

(Androcles, behind him, motions for Isabella to begin the trick).

ISABELLA *(Accepts handkerchief with a nod).* The night is so warm. The air is so still, so stifling. There is no breeze.

CAPTAIN. I will command the wind to blow a gale.

ISABELLA. The heat is so oppressive.

CAPTAIN. I will command the wind to blow a hurricane!

ANDROCLES. My nose is toasting.

CAPTAIN. I will call the wind to blow a blizzard!

ANDROCLES. My ears are roasting.

ISABELLA. The heat is baking.

(Captain, between them, looks at each one as each speaks. Captain becomes warmer and warmer. The dialogue builds slowly so the power of suggestion can take the desired effect on the Captain).

ANDROCLES. Sweltering.

ISABELLA. Smoldering.

ANDROCLES. Simmering!

ISABELLA. Seething.

(Captain begins to fan himself).

ANDROCLES. Stewing!

ISABELLA. Parching!

ANDROCLES. Scalding!

ISABELLA. Singeing!

(Captain takes off his hat, which Androcles takes, as Captain mops his brow).

ANDROCLES. Scorching!

ISABELLA. Smoking!

ANDROCLES. Sizzling!

ISABELLA. Blistering!

(Captain, growing warmer and warmer, removes his cape and sword which Androcles takes).

ANDROCLES. Broiling!

ISABELLA. Burning!

ANDROCLES. Blazing!

ISABELLA. Flaming!

CAPTAIN. Help! I am on fire! Blazing! Flaming! I am on fire!

(Captain goes in a circle, flapping his arms, puffing for air, fanning, hopping, and crying, "Fire! Fire!" At the same time, Androcles quickly gives hat, cape, sword to Isabella).

ANDROCLES *(Comes to Captain, who is slowing down)*. Throw on water! Throw on water!

CAPTAIN *(Stops, dazed)*. Where am I?

(Isabella dressed in Captain's hat, cape, and sword, marches from R and imitates Captain with comic exaggeration).

ANDROCLES *(Salutes her)*. Signor Captain! What is your philosophy for the day?

ISABELLA *(Poses and speaks in low loud voice)*. I say—he who is outside—is not inside.

ANDROCLES. Yes, my Captain.

CAPTAIN. Captain?

ISABELLA. I am off to fight a duel. Fifty-four I slew today. Fifty more I will fight—tonight!

ANDROCLES. Yes, my Captain.

CAPTAIN. Captain? Captain! *I* am the Captain.

(They pay no attention to him).

ANDROCLES. Your horse is waiting.

(Pantomimes holding a horse).

Your horse is here. Mount, O Captain, and ride away.

(Isabella pantomimes sitting on a horse, holding reins).

CAPTAIN. I am the Captain!

ISABELLA. Did you hear the wind blow?

CAPTAIN. I am the Captain!

ANDROCLES *(Listening and ignoring Captain)*. No.

ISABELLA. I will ride a thousand leagues—

ANDROCLES. Two thousand—

ISABELLA. Three—

CAPTAIN. I am the Captain!

ISABELLA. Is that a shadow—there?

(Points sword at Captain).

ANDROCLES. A shadow . . . ?

(Takes sword and slashes the air, making Captain retreat fearfully).

No one is here . . . or there . . . or anywhere.

CAPTAIN *(Almost crying).* But I am the Captain.

ANDROCLES. To horse! Away—to the woods.

ISABELLA. To the woods!

ANDROCLES. But first, a bag of stones—by the garden wall, yours to take before you go.

ISABELLA. And then—to Lelio!

ANDROCLES. Yes, my Captain.

CAPTAIN *(Crying comically).* But I am the Captain. Look at me. Listen to me.

ISABELLA. To the woods!

(Starts pantomiming riding off L).

Ride, gallop, trot, zoom!

ANDROCLES. Hop, skip—jump over the moon!

(They "ride" off U.L.)

CAPTAIN *(Crying).* But I . . . I am the Captain.

(Then horrified).

If that is the Captain—then—who—who am I?

PANTALONE *(Enters D.L.)* Captain . . . Captain.

CAPTAIN. Some one calls. Oh, Pantalone . . . Pantalone! Can you see me?

(Waves his hands in front of Pantalone, then shouts in his ear).

Can you hear me?

PANTALONE. Yes.

CAPTAIN. Am I . . . I here?

PANTALONE *(Peers at him).* Yes.

CAPTAIN. Ah, I live. I breathe again.

(Breathes vigorously).

I am the Captain.

(Struts).

Look on my hat and shudder. Look at my cape and shiver. Feel my sword—

(Realizes he has no hat, cape, or sword).

It is gone! Ah, your slave took it. Androcles! It was a trick of his. After him!

PANTALONE. My slave? Ha, ha, a trick on you.

CAPTAIN. And another one dressed in my clothes!

PANTALONE *(Laughing, stops immediately).* Another one?

CAPTAIN. One who came from your house.

PANTALONE. From my house?

(Runs to house U.R., then turns).

Isabella!

CAPTAIN. Ha ha, a trick on you.

PANTALONE *(In a rage).* Fool, stupid, simpleton! You have set Isabella free!

CAPTAIN. I let Isabella free?

PANTALONE. Fathead, saphead, noodlehead! It was she who left the house in disguise—and is off to meet her lover. Stop them! Which way? Which way?

CAPTAIN. He said—

(Thinks, which is difficult).

to the woods!

PANTALONE. Bonehead, woodenhead, block head! Quick! Save her! Before she is wed! To the woods!

(Starts R).

CAPTAIN. He said—

(Thinks).

first, take a bag of stones by the wall.

PANTALONE. A bag of stones—the gold! Muttonhead, pumpkin head, cabbage head! To the garden! Before he finds it.

(Starts to L, as Captain starts R)

Forget Isabella. Save the gold!

(Pantalone exits D.L. Captain salutes and marches after him. Lights may dim slightly. There is music as the Wall enters D.R.

24

and crosses to C. Wall is an actor (LION) with a painted "wall" hanging on his back and short enough to show his feet. The back of his head is masked by a large flower peeping over the wall. He stands at C, feet apart, back to audience. He puts down a bag of gold and then puts a rock over it.

Androcles, followed by Isabella, tiptoes in U.L. They circle around to D.R. Androcles starts feeling for the wall).

ANDROCLES.   The gold is buried—by the wall—

(Flower on the wall nods vigorously).

buried under a stone—

(Flower nods again).

Look—feel—find a stone—a stone—a stone—

(Wall stomps his foot, then puts foot on top of stone, but Androcles passes by it).

ISABELLA *(Wall again taps foot and points it towards stone. Isabella sees stone and points to it).*   A stone!

ANDROCLES.   Ah, I see it! Pray that this will be it!

(Slowly lifts stone).

Behold!

(Holds up bag).

A bag of gold!

(Jumps up, sings and dances).

We've found it! We've found it! We've found the gold! Yours to keep! To have! To hold!

ISABELLA.   Sh!

ANDROCLES.   You are free—go! Off to Lelio, who implores you— adores you. Quick, do not hesitate. Run—before it is too late.

ISABELLA.   Thank you. Some day may you be set free, too.

(Kisses her finger and touches his nose with it).

Good bye.

(Exits D.L.)

ANDROCLES *(Thrilled that she has touched him).* Fly—arreviderci.

(Sees he has the gold).

Wait! The gold! Isabella forgot the gold! Isabella! Isabella!

(He exits after her D.L. At the same time, Pantalone, followed by Captain, tip-toes in U.L., circling D.R. where they stop).

PANTALONE *(Peering and groping)*. It is so dark I cannot see.

CAPTAIN *(Also peering and groping)*. Wait . . . wait for me.

PANTALONE. The gold—by the wall—under a stone—find—find—

CAPTAIN. You look in front. I'll look behind.

PANTALONE *(He turns R, Captain turns L. Each peers and steps in the opposite direction on each word)*. Search—scratch—dig around it.

CAPTAIN *(Still peering, they now step backwards toward each other on each word)*. Feel—touch—crouch—

(They bump into each other from the back).

PANTALONE. Ouch!

CAPTAIN *(Grabs and holds Pantalone's foot)*. I've found it! I've found it!

PANTALONE. Knucklehead of soot! You've found my foot!

(Kicks free and creeps toward C).

Here . . . there . . . oh, where . . . where is my gold? The stone . . . the stone . . . where has it flown? Quick . . . on your knees . . . search . . . find . . . use your nose . . . and not to sneeze.

(He and Captain, on their knees, comically search frantically).

Pat . . . pound . . . comb . . . the ground . . . chase . . . race . . . find the place.

(He finds stone).

I have found it! Ah, to gods in prayer I kneel. The stone is here. My gold is back.

(Reaches between feet of Wall, then freezes in panic).

What do I feel? There is no sack!

(Rises in a frenzy).

I have been robbed! Thieves! The gold is gone!

CAPTAIN *(Rises)*. It was the slave who took it! Androcles!

PANTALONE. He is a robber. He is a thief! He will pay for this— with his life!

CAPTAIN. I will find him . . . bind him . . . bend . . . make an end of him!

PANTALONE. He has run away! To the woods! Catch him! Hold!

(Captain stomps to R).

To the woods! Before his tracks are cold.

(Captain stomps to L).

26

Follow! Follow! My bag of gold!

(Pantalone exits D.L. Captain salutes and follows him. Wall picks up stone, then he pulls the street scene curtain to one side, revealing another curtain behind it and painted like a forest. Over his shoulder, back still to audience, Wall announces, "The forest," and exits quickly at R.

Chase music begins. Isabella and Lelio run in from L, look about).

ISABELLA. The forest paths will guide us.

LELIO. The forest trees will hide us.

(They exit U.R. around the backdrop).

ANDROCLES *(Runs in front L)* Isabella! Lelio! I cannot find you. You have left the gold behind you.

(Exits off U.R. around backdrop).

CAPTAIN *(Enters D.L.).* After them! I say—follow me! This way!

(Exits U.R. behind backdrop).

PANTALONE *(Enters, wheezing, trying to keep up, from L).* We are near him. I can hear him—and my gold.

(Pantalone exits U.R. around the backdrop. Isabella and Lelio run in U.L. from behind the backdrop, start to R, but suddenly stop frightened at what they see offstage R).

ISABELLA. Oh, what do I see?

LELIO. It is a — quick! We must flee!

(Isabella and Lelio exit U.R. behind the backdrop. Captain enters ᵀʲ.L. around the backdrop, starts to R).

CAPTAIN This way! This way! Follow me! Onward to—

(Stops horrified at what he sees off-stage R).

What is that behind a tree? It is a—Oh, no! We must never meet. The order is—retreat!

(Captain runs off U.R. behind backdrop. Pantalone enters U.L. around the backdrop).

PANTALONE. Find him. Fetch him. Catch him. My gold has run away.

(Stops and looks off-stage R).

What is that? Can that be he?

(Starts to call).

Andro—No! It is a—Help! It is a *lion*—coming after me!

(There is a loud roar off R. Pantalone sinks to his knees and quickly walking on his knees, exits L.

27

Music of Lion's song. Lion enters at R, a most appealing creature. he dances to C and SINGS).

LION. Have you roared today,
    Told the world today how you feel?
    If you're down at the heel
    Or need to put over a deal,
    Happy or sad
    Tearful or glad
    Sunny or mad,
    It's a great way
    To show the world how you feel!
    Without saying a single word
    Your meaning is heard,
    "Good morning" is dull,
    But a roar is musical!
    Happy or sad
    Tearful or glad
    It's a great way
    To show the world how you feel!

(He gives a satisfied low roar, then looks about and speaks).

The sun is up. It is another day—

(Yawns).

to sleep. Hear all! The King speaks. No birds are allowed over my cave—chirping and burping. No animals are allowed near my cave—growling and howling. Silence in the woods. The King is going to sleep.

(Actors off-stage imitate animal sounds, loud buzzing, barking, etc. Or actors may in simple disguise with masks enter as animals, dance and make sounds).

Silence!

(All noise and motion stops).

The King says, "Silence."

(Noise and motion increases, Lion becomes angry, puffs up and roars like thunder, stalking about in all directions).

R-r-r-r-r-roar!

(There is absolute silence. If actors are on stage, they run off).

You see—

(SINGS).

A roar's a great way
To show the world how you feel!

(He roars and exits majestically into cave—a split in the painted backdrop).

28

ANDROCLES (*Enters from around backdrop U.R. He runs to C. He looks anxiously to R and to L, and calls softly*). Isabella . . . ? Lelio . . . ? They are lost in the woods. *I* am lost in the woods. I have run this way—I have run that way—I have run—

(*A terrible thought strikes him*).

I have run—away! I am a run-away slave! No!

(*Calls desperately*).

Isabella! Lelio! Where will I go? My master will hunt me. He will track me down. He will take me back. I will be thrown to the wild beasts!

(*Sees bag he holds*).

The gold—my master will say I stole it. A run-away slave—and a thief! No, I was only trying to help.

(*calls*).

Isabella! Help *me*, Lelio.

PANTALONE (*Off L, loudly*). Oh, beat the bushes. Beat the ground. Find my slave. Find my gold!

ANDROCLES. My master! What shall I do? Where shall I go? Hide—

(*Runs behind imaginary tree R*).

Behind a tree—

(*Runs to imaginary bush U.L.*)

Under a bush—he can see.

(*Points at cave*).

What is that? Ah, a cave! I will hide—inside the cave and pray he never finds me.

(*Quickly he goes into cave, gives a loud "Oh!," and quickly backs out again*).

It is someone's house.

CAPTAIN (*Off*). Follow me. I say—this way!

ANDROCLES (*Knocks at cave in desperation*). Please! Please, may I come in? I am—

PANTALONE (*Off*). I think—I hear him!

ANDROCLES. I am—in danger.

(*Androcles quickly goes into cave. Pantalone enters U.L. followed by Captain. They are in hot pursuit*).

PANTALONE (*Crosses to R*). My gold! Find the slave. Bind him! Bring him to me.

CAPTAIN *(Circles D.C.).* I will look in every brook and nook and hollow tree!

PANTALONE. Fetch—catch my gold!

(Exits D.R.).

CAPTAIN. Follow me!

(He exits D.L. From inside the cave, a long loud roar is heard, and Androcles calls, "Help!" Another and louder roar is heard. Androcles runs out of cave to D.L. and cries "Help . . . help!" Lion runs out of cave to D.R. and roars).

ANDROCLES. It is a lion!

LION. It is a man! He will try to beat me.

ANDROCLES. He will try to eat me.

(They eye each other. Lion springs at Androcles with a roar. Androcles backs away).

I am sorry I disturbed you.

(Lion roars. Androcles holds up bag).

I—I will have to hit you if you come closer.

LION. Hit—hit until he kills—that is man.

ANDROCLES. Leap—eat—that is a lion.

(Lion roars and then leaps on him. Androcles struggles and fights, but soon he is held in a lion-hug).

Help! Help!

(Lion roars. Androcles gets his arm free and bangs Lion on the back with bag of gold. Lion roars with surprise and releases Androcles. Androcles, thinking he is free, starts off, but Lion holds on to his pants. Androcles, at arm's length, runs in one spot. Androcles gets loose, turns, lowers his head and charges, butting into Lion's stomach. Lion roars. Androcles runs to L and hides behind imaginary tree. Lion, angry, roars and slowly starts to creep up on him. Androcles looks around "tree," one side, then the other, shaking with fearful expectation. Lion springs at him in front of "tree." Androcles leaps and runs back of "tree." Lion turns and runs after him. Androcles tries to escape, running in figure-eights around the two "trees." They stop, each facing opposite directions, and start backing toward each other. Androcles turns, sees Lion, jumps, then cautiously tip toes toward him and kicks the bent over approaching Lion. Lion roars and circles. Androcles laughs at his trick. Lion comes up behind him and grabs him, holding Androcles around the waist and lifting him off the ground. Androcles kicks helplessly. Lion throws Androcles on ground. Lion, above him, roars, raises his paw, and gives a crushing blow. But Androcles rolls over and the paw hits the ground. Lion immediately roars

30

and waves his paw in pain. Androcles cautiously slides away and is ready to run. He looks back at Lion who, with tearful sob-roars, is licking and waving his paw).

ANDROCLES. He is hurt. I can run away.

(He starts, but stops when Lion sobs).

He is in pain. Someone should help. No one is here. No one but one—*I*—am here.

(Lion roars in frustration. Androcles turns away in fear. Lion sobs sadly. Androcles looks back at him).

If I go—I maybe can be free! If I stay—

(Lion growls at him).

he may take a bite out of me!

(Androcles starts to leave. Lion sobs. Throughout the scene the Lion "talks" in grunts and groans almost like a person in answering and reacting to Androcles. Androcles stops).

When someone needs your help, you can't run away.

(Trying to be brave, he turns to Lion, opens his mouth, but can say nothing).

I wonder what you say—to a lion?

(Lion sobs appealingly).

Signor—

(Lion looks at him. Androcles is afraid).

My name is Androcles.

(Lion roars, looks at his paw and roars louder).

Have you—have you hurt your paw?

(Lion grunts and nods).

If you—will sit still—I will try to help you.

(Lion roars defiantly. Androcles backs away).

Wait! If we succeed, we will need to—cooperate!

(Lion looks at him suspiciously and grunts).

You don't trust me—

(Lion roars).

and I don't trust you. But someone must take the first step— greet the other, or we will never meet each other.

(Cautiously Androcles takes a step sideways, facing audience. Lion cautiously takes a step sideways, facing audience).

31

That is a beginning—

(Lion roars. Androcles holds his neck).

But what will be the ending?

(Each raises a leg and takes another sideways step toward each other).

I don't want to hurt you. I want to help you.

(He slowly holds out his hand. Lion "talks" and slowly shows him his paw).

It's a thorn. You have a thorn stuck in your paw.

(Lion breaks the tension, crying with the thought of it and waving his injured paw).

I know it hurts.

(Talks slowly as if explaining to a small child).

Once I stepped on a thorn. My father pulled it out.

(Lion grunts and reacts with interest).

My father—on the farm—by the sea. I will pull it out for you—as my father did—for me.

(Lion grunts undecided, then slowly offers his paw. Androcles nervously reaches for it).

It—it may hurt a little.

(Lion draws back and roars in protest).

I thought a lion was brave—not afraid of anything.

(Lion stops, then grunts in agreement and with great bravery thrusts out his paw).

Now—hold still—brace yourself.

(Lion begins to tremble violently).

Get ready—

(Lion shakes more).

One—

(Lion shakes both of them).

Two—

(Lion cries and tries to pull away. Androcles is stern, with pointed finger).

Don't move about!

(Lion tries to obey, meekly).

Three!

(*Lion steps backwards*).

It's out!

LION (*Looks at his paw, looks at Androcles, then roars joyfully and hops about. SINGS*).

Let me roar today
Let me say today
We feel great!
Celebrate!
Exhilarate!
Congratulate!
It's a great way
To show the world how you feel.

ANDROCLES (*Lion rubs against Androcles and purrs softly. Androcles, being tickled by Lion's rubbing, giggles and pets him*). You—you are welcome.

LION (*To audience*). He looks tired. I will get a rock.

(*Quickly picks up a rock off R and holds it high*).

ANDROCLES. He is going to crush me!

(*He starts to defend himself, but Lion shakes his head and grunts, and shows Androcles that he should sit*).

For me?

(*Lion nods, trying to talk, and dusts the rock with his tail*).

He wants *me* to sit.

(*Lion, delighted, grabs Androcles to help him and seats him roughly*).

Thank you.

LION (*To audience*). He looks hungry.

(*Roars, shows teeth, and chews*).

ANDROCLES. He is going to eat me!

(*Lion shakes his head and "talks," points to Androcles and indicates from his mouth down into his stomach*).

He wants *me* to eat.

(*Lion agrees joyfully*).

I am hungry. I am always hungry.

LION. (*Thinking*). What was for breakfast today? A man's skull in the cave—his liver down by the river—

(*Embarrassed at what he has thought*).

33

Oh, I beg your pardon.

(Roars with a new idea, motions Androcles to watch. Lion hums and purrs lightly as he comically pantomimes picking fruit from a tree and eating and spitting out the seeds).

ANDROCLES. Fruit!

(Lion, encouraged, purrs happily and hops about pantomiming filling a basket with berries from bushes).

Berries!

(Lion, elated with his success, buzzes loudly and dances in ballet fashion like a bee).

What?

(Lion buzzes and dances bigger).

Honey from the bee!

(Lion agrees loudly).

Oh, that will be a banquet for me.

LION *(Speaks to audience).* A new twist in history! Man and beast will feast together. Celebrate! Sit—wait! I'll be back with cherries and berries for you—and a bone or two, before you can roar —e pluribus unum!

(Roars happily and exits R).

ANDROCLES *(Sits alone on rock, looks around, smiles, and speaks quietly).* I am sitting down. I am being served. I am being treated like a person. I—have a friend. This is what it is like to be free. To be—maybe—

(SINGS).

Maybe
A doctor with a degree,
A poet, a priest, a sculptor, a scholar,
A senator—emperor with a golden collar!
I want to be free
So I can find—me.

PANTALONE *(Off).* Hunt—hunt—search and find my slave. Find my gold!

ANDROCLES. My master has come. My freedom has gone.

PANTALONE *(Off R).* Ah, his footprints are on the ground! I have found him!

ANDROCLES *(Calls quickly).* Oh, Lion, I must be off before we have fed. I must run—or it is off with my head!

(He starts D.L. but sees Captain).

Oh! The Captain! Where will I hide? In the cave!

(Quickly hides in cave).

CAPTAIN *(Enters L with fishing net and a slap-stick).* Beware slave, wherever you are. I shall leap and keep and capture you. In this net—I will get you.

(Holds net out ready).

PANTALONE *(Enters R, peering at the ground, crosses to L).* His footprints are on the ground. Toe-heel, heel-toe. This is the way his footsteps go.

CAPTAIN *(To audience).* The trap is set.

PANTALONE. Lead on—lead me to him.

CAPTAIN. Ha, caught in the net!

(Throws net over Pantalone who has walked into it).

PANTALONE. Help! Help!

CAPTAIN. You stole my hat!

(Hits Pantalone over the head with slap-stick).

PANTALONE. Oh!

CAPTAIN. My sword.

(Hits him again).

PANTALONE. No!

CAPTAIN. My cape!

(Hits him again).

PANTALONE. Let me loose!

CAPTAIN. What?

PANTALONE. You squawking goose!

CAPTAIN. Who speaks?

PANTALONE *(Pulling off the net).* I—Pantalone.

CAPTAIN. Pantalone? Oh, it was my mistake.

PANTALONE. It was my head!

CAPTAIN. Where is the slave? The runaway? Where is Androcles?

PANTALONE. He is—with my gold.

CAPTAIN *(Struts).* I will drag him back to Rome. The Emperor will honor me—decree a holiday—so all can see the slave fight a wild and hungry beast. And after the fun is done and the slave is eaten, all will cheer the Captain of the Year.

35

PANTALONE. Before you count your cheers, you have to catch one slave—Androcles!

CAPTAIN *(They start searching, a step on each word. Captain circles to L and upstage. Pantalone circles to R and upstage).* Search.

PANTALONE. Seek.

CAPTAIN. Track.

PANTALONE. Trail.

CAPTAIN. Use your eyes.

PANTALONE. Scrutinize!

CAPTAIN *(Stops).* Think—if you were a slave . . . ?

PANTALONE. I?

CAPTAIN. Where would you hide?

PANTALONE. Inside.

CAPTAIN *(Sees and points).* A cave!

(They tip-toe to entrance, hold net ready, whisper excitedly).

Clap him.

PANTALONE. Trap him.

CAPTAIN *(Nothing happens).* The problem is—how to get him to come out.

PANTALONE. Poke him?

CAPTAIN. Smoke him?

PANTALONE. I have a great idea! You will call to him in a voice like Isabella.

CAPTAIN. I—I speak like Isabella?

PANTALONE. You will cry for help in a soft sweet voice. He will think you are her. He will come to Isabella.

CAPTAIN *(In high voice, comically).* Help! Oh, help me. I am Isabella.

(They look at cave entrance).

I heard—

PANTALONE. Something stirred.

CAPTAIN *(Falsetto again).* Andro-o-cles. Come out, ple-e-ese.

(They look at cave and excitedly hold net ready).

Ready.

PANTALONE. Steady.

(Androcles, behind backdrop, roars—long and loud!).

It is a lion in the cave!

(Runs D.R. and hides behind a "tree").

CAPTAIN *(Androcles roars again, up and down the scale, louder and louder. Even the backdrop shakes. Captain jumps and runs to Pantalone and hides behind him).* It is two lions in the cave!

(They stand shaking with fright).

ANDROCLES *(Peeks out of cave, then comes out).* They have gone. Ran away from a noise. I have learned that a roar is a mighty thing. No wonder a lion is a king.

(He enjoys another roar).

PANTALONE *(Still hiding).* We are undone!

CAPTAIN. Run! Crawl!

PANTALONE. I cannot move at all.

(Androcles roars again with joy).

I have an idea. You—you will call in a voice like a lion. He will think you are another lion—a brother.

CAPTAIN. I—roar like a lion?

PANTALONE. Our only chance is to answer back.

(Captain gulps, and then roars).

ANDROCLES *(He is startled. He hides behind "tree" at L).* It is another lion.

(Pantalone, helping, gives a roar).

It is two lions!

(With an idea, he roars back).

Ro-o-o-hello.

CAPTAIN *(He and Pantalone look at each other in surprise. Captain answers).* Ro-o-o-hello.

ANDROCLES *(Now Androcles looks surprised).* Ro-o-o-lovely-da-a-ay.

CAPTAIN *(He and Pantalone look at each other and nod, pleased with their success).* Ro-o o-have-you-seen—ro-o-o-ar-a-runaway slave?

(Androcles is startled, then he peeks around "tree").

PANTALONE. Named-Andro—

(Captain nudges him to roar).

—roar—cles?

ANDROCLES. It is my master and the Captain. They have come for me.

(He roars loudly).

Ro-o-oar-he-went—roar-r-r-r-that-away.

CAPTAIN *(They nod).* Ro-o-o-thank-you.

(He and Pantalone start to tip-toe off R).

ANDROCLES *(Too confident).* Ro—o-ar. You are welcome.

PANTALONE. It is his voice. It is my slave, Androcles.

CAPTAIN. It is another trick of his.

PANTALONE. Nab him.

CAPTAIN. Grab him.

(They start back to get him).

ANDROCLES *(Unaware he has been discovered, continues to roar gaily).* Ro-o-oar. Goodbye. Ro-o-o-ar. Happy eating.

PANTALONE *(Confronts Androcles on R).* Eat, cheat, thief! I will beat you!

(Androcles turns to L and walks into net held by Captain).

CAPTAIN. Slide, glide, inside. I have you tied!

(Androcles is caught in the net over his head).

PANTALONE *(Grabs his bag of gold).* My gold!

CAPTAIN. My captive!

ANDROCLES. Help! Help!

CAPTAIN. You stole my hat!

(Hits Androcles over the head with slap-stick).

You stole my sword!

(Hits him).

You stole my cape!

(Hits him).

This time you will not escape.

PANTALONE *(Takes stick from Captain and swings it).* Robber, Traitor. Thief! Let me hit him.

(Pantalone, in the mix up, hits Captain several times on his head).

CAPTAIN. Help!

(He drops the rope of the net).

38

ANDROCLES *(Runs to R)*. Help!

PANTALONE. Help! He is running away!

CAPTAIN *(Quickly catches Androcles and holds the rope)*. Back to Rome. To the Emperor you will be delivered!

PANTALONE. Into the pit you will be thrown.

CAPTAIN. Where the wild beasts will claw, gnaw, and chew you!

(They start to lead him off, marching—Captain, Androcles, and last Pantalone).

Munch!

PANTALONE. Crunch!

ANDROCLES. I will be eaten for lunch! Help! Lion! Signor Lion, set me free. Come and rescue me! Oh, woods echo my cry for help. Echo so the Lion will know I am in trouble. Roar—roar with me. Echo from tree to tree!

(He roars and the Ushers—and the children—help him roar, as he is led off L).

Roar! Roar!

LION *(He leaps in at R and roars)*. Someone roars for help? Androcles!

(Off, Androcles cries "Help!")

He calls for help.

(SINGS).

Oh, roar and say
Shout out without delay,
Which way, which way, which way?
Oh, roar me a clue,
Roar me two.
I have to know
Which way to go before I start.
Oh, roar, please,
An-dro-cles.
Give a sigh,
Give a cry,
Signify!
I'll sniff—I'll whiff—
Smell *(Sniffs)* — Tell *(Sniffs)*
Fe, fi, fo, fum.
Here —

(Shouts).

I come!

(He exits L).

39

ISABELLA *(She and Lelio run in from R).* Oh, Androcles, what has happened to you?

LELIO *(To audience).* That you will see in Act Two. Now—we must bow and say, "Our play is half done." This is the end of Act One.

(They bow).

The Curtains Close.

A short intermission.

(Or if played without an intermission, omit the last speech of Lelio's and continue with his first speech in Act Two).

From New York production of ANDROCLES AND THE LION

ANDROCLES AND THE LION

ACT TWO

(Music: Reprise of "Oh, Roar and Say." The curtains open. The scene is the same. Isabella and Lelio stand in C. Music dims out).

ISABELLA. Androcles. What has happened to you?

LELIO. I heard his voice, calling in the woods.

ISABELLA. He has followed us to bring the gold—my dowry which I left behind.

(Calls).

Androcles?

LELIO. Androcles!

(Lion roars as he enters U.R. He sees the lovers and watches).

ISABELLA. It is a lion!

LELIO. Do not fear.

ISABELLA. Androcles is alone—unarmed. What if he should meet a lion? Androcles! Androcles!

LELIO. Androcles!

LION. Someone else roars "Androcles." I will stay and hear who is here.

(Lion hides his head behind the small rock).

ISABELLA. Androcles! Androcles!

LELIO. We are alone.

(Lion's head pops up behind rock).

Together. It is the time to speak—to sing of love!

(He turns aside, takes scroll from belt).

ISABELLA *(Not looking at him).* Please, speak no prepared speech, but sing true words that spring freely from your heart.

41

LELIO *(Looks surprised, glances again at scroll, then SINGS).*

Oh, lovely, lovely flower,
Growing lovelier every hour,
Shower on me, petals of love, Isabella—

(Lion, enjoying the music, nods his head in rhythm).

ISABELLA. So unrehearsed—so sincere.

LELIO *(SINGS).*

My life, my heart revolve about you.
Say yes, I cannot live without you.

(Lion, unable to refrain, lifts his head and roars musically on Lelio's last note—unnoticed by the lovers—then hides his head behind the rock).

ISABELLA. Oh, Lelio—

(Turns to him and speaks or SINGS).

My answer is—can't you guess?
Yes, yes, yes, yes, yes!

LELIO *(In ecstacy).* Oh, woods abound with joyous sound! Melodies sing in the trees—

(Music sound. Lion raises up and listens to R).

Bells ring in the breeze—

(Music sound. Lion stands up and listens to L).

Let the lute of the lily lying in the pond—

(Music sound. Lion stands and begins to move his arms like an orchestra conductor).

Let the flute of the firefly's fluttering wand—

(Music sound. Lion motions to R).

And let the flight of the nightingale—

(Music sound. Lion motions L).

Harmonize!

(Music sounds blend together. Lion holds up paw ready to begin directing an orchestra).

The moment we will immortalize!

(Music of all sounds play a folk dance. Lion leads, dramatically, the unseen musicians. Isabella and Lelio do a short dance. At the conclusion, they hold their pose and Lion bows to audience).

ISABELLA *(Points to ground).* Look! Footprints—boots and sandals.

LELIO *(Examines them).* The Captain's boots—Pantalone's sandals.

The Captain and Pantalone were here—following us—following Androcles.

ISABELLA. His cry was for help. He ran away. He is—a runaway slave! And they have found him—

LELIO. Bound him—

ISABELLA. Taken him back to Rome.

LELIO. To the pit!

ISABELLA. We must stop them.

LELIO. If we can.

ISABELLA. We must help him.

LELIO. All we can.

LION (Jumps on rock heroically). And—we can!

(Roars).

ISABELLA. Help!

LELIO. Run!

(Lovers run off D.R.).

LION. Lead the way. I will follow you. To Androcles! To—the rescue!

(Lion roars, picks up rock, and runs off D.R. Chase music begins —repeated. But the running is reversed, going around in the opposite direction. Lovers enter from U.R. and run across. At C, they look back, "Oh!" and exit U.L. behind backdrop. Lion runs in U.R. At C, roars, and exits U.L. behind backdrop. Lovers enter U.R. from behind backdrop, running faster. At C, they look back in great fright, "OH!" and exit U.L. behind backdrop. Lion follows. At C, roars majestically, and shouts: "Andr—roar—cles! Here we come!" Lion exits after lovers. Lovers enter U.R. from around backdrop. Lelio pulls the curtain of the woods scene back to L, showing the street scene again. Chase music dims out).

LELIO (Breathless). Safe at home—I hope. What does the scroll say?

ISABELLA (Reads scroll on proscenium arch). The next scene is—a street in Rome.

LELIO. Ah, we can stay.

ISABELLA (Reads, announcing). "The Captain enters."

(Clashing of slap-stick is heard off L, Isabella runs to C).

He will find us here.

LELIO. Do not fear. We will hide—behind a mask. Quick! We will hide behind another face, and re-appear in the Market Place.

(They exit R).

43

CAPTAIN (*Enters at L*). Make way, make way for the hero of the day! Bow, salute, kneel and gaze upon the hero. Raise your voice with praise for the hero. The hero passes by. The hero is—I!

(*Lelio and Isabella enter R. Each holds a long, sad beggerman's mask on a stick in front of his face. They walk and act and speak like beggars*).

LELIO. Help the poor. Help the blind.

ISABELLA. Alms for the cripple. Alms for the old.

CAPTAIN. Away beggars! The Emperor comes this way. It is a holiday!

LELIO. What Senator has died? What battle have we won?

CAPTAIN. None! We celebrate today the capture of a runaway.

ISABELLA. A slave?

(*They look at each other and speak without their masks; and at the same time, the Captain speaks. They all say together, "Androcles!"*).

CAPTAIN. Today all Rome will celebrate! A wild beast was caught outside the wall, clawing the gate as if he could not wait to come into the City. Now in the pit the beast is locked and barred, waiting to be released—waiting to eat a juicy feast.

LELIO AND ISABELLA (*They nod to each other and say:*) Androcles!

CAPTAIN. Ah, what a sporting sight to see—a fight—man eaten by a beast. Then I, who caught the slave, will appear. Women will swoon, men will cheer, and I will be crowned the hero of the year!

(*Shouts rapidly and marches quickly*).

Hep, hep, ho! Step, step, high. Hail the hero. I, I, I!

(*Exits R*).

ISABELLA (*They take their masks away*). Poor, poor Androcles.

LELIO. We must try and save him. Quick, before it is too late. We will go to the Arena—

ISABELLA. Yes!

LELIO. We will go to the Royal Box! Implore the Emperor with our plea!

ISABELLA. Yes!

LELIO. For only he by royal decree can save—our Androcles.

(*Lelio and Isabella run off L. There is music. Captain, leading Androcles by the rope, and Pantalone following, marches in from R. As they march, they SING*).

44

PANTALONE AND CAPTAIN. Off to the pit we three. Who will be left?

ANDROCLES. Just me.

PANTALONE AND CAPTAIN. Who will be left alone, shaking in every bone?

PANTALONE. Just—

CAPTAIN. Just—

ANDROCLES. Me!

CAPTAIN AND PANTALONE. Off to the pit we three. Who will be left?

ANDROCLES. Just me.

CAPTAIN AND PANTALONE. Who will the animal meet? Who will the animal eat?

PANTALONE. Just—

CAPTAIN. Just—

ANDROCLES *(Shouts).* Just a minute! I want to be an absentee!

(Music ends as he speaks).

I want to be free—to be—just me!

CAPTAIN. To the Arena! Forward march!

(Music: Reprise of Introductory Music of Act One. Captain, Androcles, and Pantalone march across the front of the stage or across down in the orchestra pit. At the same time, Lelio and Isabella, disguised with masks, dance in U.L. carrying colorful banners, one in each hand, and on stands. They set the banners down in a semi-circle in front of the backdrop to indicate the Arena. They dance off as the music stops, and the three marchers arrive in the middle of the scene).

CAPTAIN. Halt! We are at the Arena! The slave will step forward.

PANTALONE. Step forward.

ANDROCLES. Step forward.

(Frightened, he steps forward).

CAPTAIN. The slave's head will be covered.

(He holds out left hand to Androcles, who holds out left hand to Pantalone).

PANTALONE. Covered.

(He gives a cloth sack to Androcles, who gives it to Captain, who puts it over Androcles' head).

CAPTAIN *(Trumpets sound).* The Emperor's chariot draws near.

(Trumpets).

45

The Emperor will soon appear.

(Trumpets).

The Emperor is here!

(A royal banner is extended from the side D.L., indicating the Royal Box).

Bow!

PANTALONE. Now!

(Captain and Pantalone bow low toward Royal Box, facing D.L. Androcles groping with his head covered, turns and bows facing R).

Turn around!

(Androcles turns around).

To the ground!

(Androcles bows to ground).

CAPTAIN. Most noble Emperor—

(Pushes Androcles' head down, making him bow).

Most honored Emperor—

(Pushes Androcles, who keeps bobbing up, down again).

Most imperial Emperor—

(Pushes Androcles down again. He stays down).

The guilty slave stands before you. Stand!

(Androcles quickly straightens up).

As punishment for a slave who runs away, he will today fight a wild beast in the Arena for all Rome to see.

(Androcles shakes his head under the sack).

He will battle for his life—to survive. There will be but one winner—the one who is left alive.

(Androcles, courageously, draws his fists and is ready to strike. Captain, growing more eloquent, begins to strut).

I have fought and slain a hundred wild beasts.

(Androcles, visualizing the animals, starts hitting the air).

With fiery eyes, with gnashing teeth, they charged at me. Fight! The crowd cried, fight!

(Androcles, ready, starts to fight, hitting wildly for his life, hitting the Captain who is near and whom he cannot see).

Help! Stop! I am not the wild beast.

(At a safe distance, he regains his bravery).

46

I—I am the Captain, the boldest, bravest fighter in Rome—in all Italy! Go—stand at the side. Appear when you hear the trumpets blow.

(Captain points to L. Androcles starts to R).

No. The other way!

ANDROCLES *(He turns and starts to L. Loud trumpets blow. He stops, faces R, ready to fight).* The trumpets! Now?

PANTALONE. No!

(Androcles, groping, exits U.L. Pantalone bows to Royal Box).

Most Imperial Emperor, I am Pantalone, Master of the slave. From me he ran away. From me he stole. I am told you plan to reward me for this holiday with a bag of gold.

CAPTAIN. I tracked and captured him. I am sure you will confer a title of bravery on me.

(Trumpets blow).

ANDROCLES *(Enters U.L., ready to fight).* The trumpets! Now?

CAPTAIN. No!

(Androcles turns and exits).

Ah, the Emperor waves. It is the signal. Open the gates. Let the wild beast in!

PANTALONE. Let the entertainment begin!

(Captain and Pantalone quickly go D.R. where they stand. Drum rolls are heard. Then loud roars are heard off U.R. Lion, roaring, angrily stalks in from U.R.).

LION. Barred—locked—caged! I am—outraged!

(Roars and paces menacingly).

PANTALONE. What a big lion! I am glad he is below.

CAPTAIN. I could conquer him with one blow.

LION. Captured! Held in captivity! Robbed of my liberty! Only man would think of it. Only man would sink to it. Man—man— little—two legged—tailless thing. Beware man, I am a King!

(Roars).

The first man I meet I—will eat!

(Trumpets blow).

ANDROCLES *(Enters, head still covered).* The trumpets! Now?

LION *(Sees him).* Ah, a man! A chew or two and a bone to pick.

(Roars).

47

ANDROCLES (*Frightened and groping*). Oh! I am not alone. I must get out quick.

(*Drum starts beating in rhythm to the fight. Androcles starts walking, then running, the Lion after him. The chase is a dance-mime, fast, comic, with surprises and suspense. It ends with Lion holding Androcles in his clutches*).

LION. Caught! Held!

(*Shakes Androcles like a rag doll*).

Flip—flop. I will start eating at the top!

(*Takes off Androcles' headcovering*).

ANDROCLES. No hope ever to be free. This is the end of me!

(*Lion looks at Androcles, is surprised and roars questioningly. Androcles, frightened, freezes, then slowly feels his neck, his face and nose. He looks at Lion and he is surprised. Lion tries to "talk"*).

You?

(*Lion nods and roars, pantomimes pulling out a thorn from his paw, and points to Androcles who nods*).

Me.

(*Lion "talks" and points to himself*).

You!

(*Lion nods and roars happily*).

Signor Lion!

(*Lion "talks" and roars, and they embrace each other joyfully*).

PANTALONE. Let the fight begin! Beat him!

(*Lion stops and looks at Pantalone*).

CAPTAIN. The Emperor waits to see who wins. Eat him!

ANDROCLES. He is my master—who bought me. He is the Captain—who caught me.

LION. Slave makers! Taker of men! I will beat you! I will eat you!

(*Roars and starts to C*).

PANTALONE. Help! The lion is looking at me. Draw your sword!

(*Hides behind the Captain*).

CAPTAIN (*Shaking*). I am afraid his blood will rust the blade.

PANTALONE. Show you can do what you say—slay him with one blow!

CAPTAIN. I suddenly remember—I have to go!

(Starts off R. At the same time, Lion leaps with a roar and attacks the two).

PANTALONE. Help! Guards! Save, attend me!

CAPTAIN. Help! Someone defend me!

(There is an exciting and comic scramble, with Lion finally grabbing each by the collar and hitting their heads together. Then he holds each out at arms length).

LION. Listen and learn a lesson: only a coward steals and holds a man.

(Roars. Shakes Pantalone).

Only a thief buys and sells a man. And no one—can—own another man!

(Roars).

The world was made for all—equally. Nod your heads if you agree.

(Lion shakes them and makes their heads nod violently. Then he releases them, and the two drop to the ground).

The vote is "Yes"—unanimously!

(Trumpets sound. Off-stage voices shout, from R and L and from the back of the auditorium: "Kill the lion. The lion is loose. Club him. Stone him. Kill the lion. Kill! Kill! etc." Captain and Pantalone crawl to R. Hands appear off R and L shaking clubs and spears. This is a tense moment. The Arena has turned against the Lion. Lion is frightened. He crouches by Androcles who stands heroically by him).

ANDROCLES. Stop! Stop! Hold your spears and stones and clubs. Do not kill the lion. You see—he is not an enemy. He remembers me and a kindness which I did for him. Today that kindness he has returned. He did not eat my head, which would have been the end. Instead—he is—my friend.

(He offers his hand to Lion. Lion takes it. Music begins and the two start to waltz together. Pantalone and Captain crouch and watch in amazement. Hands and weapons disappear from the sides at R and L. Androcles and Lion waltz bigger, funnier, and happier. Trumpets sound. Music and dancing stop. Lelio enters D.L. by royal banner).

LELIO. The Emperor has spoken. His words will be heard.

(All bow low toward the Box as Lelio holds up a royal scroll).

The Emperor is amazed, astounded, and astonished—with delight —at this sudden sight. A fight unlike any in history. Indeed it is a mystery. Two enemies—man and lion—dancing hand in hand! To honor this unique occasion, the Emperor has issued this command: today shall be, not one of fighting, but of dance and revelry!

49

(Trumpets play and people cheer).

The Emperor gives to the Master of the slave—

PANTALONE. That is I, Pantalone. How much gold does he give?

LELIO. The Emperor gives this order; *you* will give twenty pieces of gold to Androcles.

ANDROCLES. To me!

LELIO. A sum he has well earned.

PANTALONE. Give twenty pieces of gold! Oh, I shall die a poor man. No. No!

(Lion starts toward him and growls loudly).

Yes—yes, I will pay.

(Quickly takes bag from pocket and begins counting).

One—two—three—

LELIO. Furthermore: the Emperor decrees to the Captain who caught the slave—

CAPTAIN. Ah, what honor does the Emperor give to me?

LELIO. You will command a Roman Legion in a distant land. You will sail to the Isle of Britain where even the boldest man must fight to keep alive, where it is so dangerous only the bravest survive.

CAPTAIN *(Shaking violently).* Danger? Fight? Me?

LELIO. Because of your boasted bravery.

CAPTAIN. I would prefer to stay, please. A cold climate makes me sneeze.

(Lion starts and roars loudly).

I will go.

(Lion follows him roaring).

I am going! I am gone!

LELIO. And to me—the Emperor has given me the lovely, lovely Isabella—

(Isabella enters D.L.).

and has blessed our marriage which soon will be.

ISABELLA. For me the Emperor decreed, Pantalone shall pay without delay my dowry which he holds for me.

PANTALONE. Pay more gold! Oh, no—no!

(Lion roars at him loudly).

50

Yes—yes. I will pay. It is here, my dear.

LELIO. And finally:

(Trumpets blow).

The Emperor has ruled that both lion and slave today have won a victory unequalled in history. So—both lion and slave are hereby —set free!

ANDROCLES. Free? I am free.

LION. The way the world should be!

ANDROCLES. Free—to find my family—to work the best I can—to raise my head—to be a man. To find out—who I am!

(Music. They all SING).

Let us roar today,
Let us say today
We feel great.
Celebrate!
Exhilarate!
Congratulate!

PANTALONE AND CAPTAIN *(Dejected).* We don't feel great.

ALL. It's a great way
To show the world how you feel.
When in need—find a friend.
Laws will read—have a friend.
We feel great.
Don't eat, but meet.
Why wait, make a friend.
Extend!
Do your part, make a start.
Roar today. Show the world today.
It's a great way
To show the world how you feel.

(All the actors bow, then Androcles comes forward).

ANDROCLES. Our story is told. The lovers are joined in happiness. The bragger and the miser are undone. And a friend was won by kindness. Our masks and bells and curtains we put away for another day. And we go our way—a group of strolling players. We say—

LION *(Points at audience).* Be sure you roar today!

ALL. Arreviderci!

(They all bow low and the music swells).

The curtains close.